God, Grant me the serenity

To accept the things I cannot change

The courage to change the things I can

The wisdom to know the difference

God, Grant me the serenity

To accept the things I cannot change

The courage to change the things I can

The wisdom to know the difference

God, Grant me the serenity

To accept the things I cannot change

The courage to change the things I can

The wisdom to know the difference

God, Grant me the serenity

To accept the things I cannot change

The courage to change the things I can

The wisdom to know the difference

God, Grant me the serenity

To accept the things I cannot change

The courage to change the things I can

The wisdom to know the difference

God, Grant me the serenity

To accept the things I cannot change

The courage to change the things I can

The wisdom to know the difference

God, Grant me the serenity

To accept the things I cannot change

The courage to change the things I can

The wisdom to know the difference

God, Grant me the serenity

To accept the things I cannot change

The courage to change the things I can

_____

_____

_____

_____

_____

_____

_____

_____

_____

_____

_____

_____

_____

_____

_____

_____

_____

The wisdom to know the difference

God, Grant me the serenity

To accept the things I cannot change

The courage to change the things I can

The wisdom to know the difference

God, Grant me the serenity

To accept the things I cannot change

The courage to change the things I can

The wisdom to know the difference

God, Grant me the serenity

To accept the things I cannot change

The courage to change the things I can

The wisdom to know the difference

God, Grant me the serenity

To accept the things I cannot change

The courage to change the things I can

The wisdom to know the difference

Made in the USA
Las Vegas, NV
17 November 2021

34617517R00057